DATE DUE

DEC			
MAR			
MAR 0	MAR 0		
OCT 2 5			
APR 2 8			
NOV 2 6			
MAY 1 3			
JAN 2			
NOV 1 9			

Demco, Inc. 38-293

CRETACEOUS DINOSAUR WORLD

Coyote Ridge Elementary School
13770 Broadlands Drive
Broomfield, CO 80020
720-872-5780

For a free color catalog describing Gareth Stevens' list of high-quality books and multimedia programs, call 1-800-542-2595 (USA) or 1-800-461-9120 (Canada). Gareth Stevens Publishing's Fax: (414) 225-0377. See our catalog, too, on the World Wide Web: gsinc.com

Library of Congress Cataloging-in-Publication Data

Green, Tamara, 1945-
   Cretaceous dinosaur world/by Tamara Green; illustrated by Richard Grant.
     p. cm. — (World of dinosaurs)
   Includes bibliographical references and index.
   Summary: Reconstructs dinosaur life during the Cretaceous period, presenting the predominant species until their ultimate demise.
   ISBN 0-8368-2173-4 (lib. bdg.)
   1. Dinosaurs—Juvenile literature. 2. Paleontology—Cretaceous—Juvenile literature. [1. Dinosaurs. 2. Paleontology.]
I. Grant, Richard, 1959- ill. II. Title. III. Series: World of dinosaurs.
QE862.D5G734825 1998
567.9—dc21   98-23074

This North American edition first published in 1998 by
Gareth Stevens Publishing
1555 North RiverCenter Drive, Suite 201
Milwaukee, Wisconsin 53212 USA

This U.S. edition © 1998 by Gareth Stevens, Inc.
Created with original © 1998 by Quartz Editorial Services,
112 Station Road, Edgware HA8 7AQ U.K.
Additional end matter © 1998 by Gareth Stevens, Inc.

Consultant: Dr. Paul Barrett, Paleontologist, Specialist in Biology and Evolution of Dinosaurs, University of Cambridge, England.

Printed in the United States of America

1 2 3 4 5 6 7 8 9 02 01 00 99 98

CRETACEOUS DINOSAUR WORLD

by Tamara Green
Illustrations by Richard Grant

Gareth Stevens Publishing
MILWAUKEE

CONTENTS

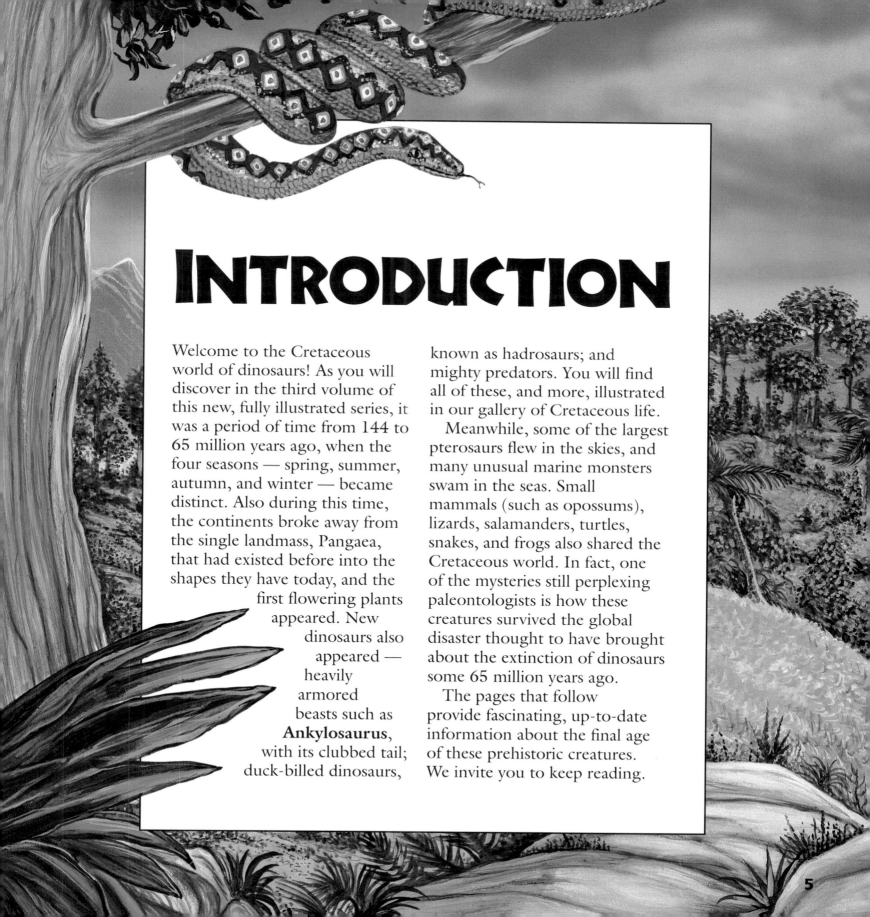

INTRODUCTION

Welcome to the Cretaceous world of dinosaurs! As you will discover in the third volume of this new, fully illustrated series, it was a period of time from 144 to 65 million years ago, when the four seasons — spring, summer, autumn, and winter — became distinct. Also during this time, the continents broke away from the single landmass, Pangaea, that had existed before into the shapes they have today, and the first flowering plants appeared. New dinosaurs also appeared — heavily armored beasts such as **Ankylosaurus**, with its clubbed tail; duck-billed dinosaurs, known as hadrosaurs; and mighty predators. You will find all of these, and more, illustrated in our gallery of Cretaceous life.

Meanwhile, some of the largest pterosaurs flew in the skies, and many unusual marine monsters swam in the seas. Small mammals (such as opossums), lizards, salamanders, turtles, snakes, and frogs also shared the Cretaceous world. In fact, one of the mysteries still perplexing paleontologists is how these creatures survived the global disaster thought to have brought about the extinction of dinosaurs some 65 million years ago.

The pages that follow provide fascinating, up-to-date information about the final age of these prehistoric creatures. We invite you to keep reading.

CRETACEOUS

Dinosaurs of all shapes and sizes populated our planet in Cretaceous times — the last and longest age of these prehistoric animals. What sort of landscape did they inhabit? What was the world like way back then?

Two handsome, crested **Parasaurolophus** (*left*) drank from a clear pool. Not far away, a lone **Ankylosaurus** (*above*) chewed on ferns and sniffed around for seeds and fruits along the shallow banks. For the moment, it was a peaceful scene. Yet it was part of the highly volatile Cretaceous world, constantly convulsed by earthquakes, floods, and volcanoes. These herbivores also had to cope with the terrifying threat of giant carnivores.

Overflowing oceans

The sea level had risen over millions of years, so that by Cretaceous times, hills and mountains were pushed up as the present-day continents drifted apart from the original, single landmass, Pangaea. Some experts have compared what happened with what occurs if you were to push up the bottom of a bathtub. The water level would rise over the rim and overflow. That is what happened as the ocean floor rose.

LANDSCAPES

Earthquakes and volcanoes were much more common on our planet at that time than they are today, and their eruptions must have killed many dinosaurs. For the first time, distinct seasons began to appear. There were fewer areas of tropical rain forest, too, and more woodland regions. These changes provided ideal conditions for insects, small mammals, and reptiles to live.

First flowering plants

At the beginning of the Cretaceous period, some 144 million years ago, conifer trees, ferns, and horsetails flourished. But the first flowering plants soon appeared, including primitive roses, magnolias, and water lilies, which were pollinated by the early butterflies, ants, wasps, and bees. Mighty oak trees and hickories also grew in the lush, green Cretaceous forests.

This may sound a lot like the landscape of Earth today but, of course, there was one huge difference — the dinosaurs! Among them were many new species that evolved during the 80 million years that Cretaceous times lasted — more species of dinosaurs than ever before.

As the continents we know today began to drift apart from the single landmass, called Pangaea, which experts believe existed on Earth before this time, some types of dinosaurs became isolated. This explains why some species have been unearthed only in localized parts of the world.

7

THE NEW PLANT-EATERS

Cretaceous times were not all blood and destruction. Herbivores were social creatures, and sticking together in groups would have protected them from predators much of the time.

During the Cretaceous period, many new species of plant-eaters appeared on Earth. Smaller and more mobile than the huge, long-necked sauropods, such as **Brachiosaurus** and **Diplodocus**, of Jurassic times, they spent most of their time peacefully munching the lush, green foliage of fertile Cretaceous lowlands.

One of the most striking-looking herbivores must have been horned **Chasmosaurus**, whose large, bony head crest was used mainly for display purposes. Solidly built and about 16 feet (5 meters) long, it inhabited what is now Canada, as well as New Mexico in the United States.

Hadrosaurus, from the same part of the world, belonged to the hadrosaur, or duck-billed group of dinosaurs, which appeared only during the Cretaceous period. It had large numbers of teeth in its ducklike mouth, ideal for grinding up huge quantities of vegetation.

Hadrosaurus grew to 30 feet (9 m) in length. Its broad tail and paddlelike hands indicate it may have run toward water when eluding predators such as **Tyrannosaurus rex**, which was deadly on land but probably a poor swimmer.

Lambeosaurus (*below, right*) had an incredible crest on its head. This crest may have been used to identify members of its species and to determine social status. **Lambeosaurus** had a sturdy body and, like other hadrosaurs, could walk on two legs or all four.

9

CRETACEOUS PREDATORS

Herbivores greatly outnumbered carnivores during this time. Although many of the plant-eating dinosaurs were protected by body armor, they never knew when a marauding meat-eater might be driven by hunger and instinct to attack.

It was a hot Cretaceous afternoon, and a young **Triceratops** stood in a clearing, idly chewing on some plants. Little did it suspect that this would be its last meal. It was about to become a meal itself, the victim of the most feared Cretaceous predator — **Tyrannosaurus rex**. When fully grown, this 39-foot (12-m)-long carnivore weighed up to 7 tons and had amazingly sharp teeth.

Although **Triceratops** was well-armed with its three tough horns and mighty neck shield, **Tyrannosaurus rex** knew that its best plan of attack was to tip **Triceratops** onto its back and expose its vulnerable belly.

Painful death

Squealing in agony as the larger dinosaur bit into its flesh, the **Triceratops** was soon totally disabled. But **Tyrannosaurus rex** would not eat immediately. It was still full from a recent snack of a few chicken-sized dinosaurs. Instead, the predator would wait a couple of hours before feasting on the carcass of its latest victim.

The Cretaceous world was home to many other predators, as well. **Spinosaurus**, found in what is now northern Africa, was as long as **Tyrannosaurus rex**. It had a remarkable sail on its back, which many scientists believe was used to control its body temperature. **Carnotaurus**, from what is now Argentina in South America, was just over half the length of **Spinosaurus** but it was still one of the most vicious predators of its time. It had broad horns that jutted out over its eyes, thus its name, meaning "meat-eating bull," and a very scaly body. All in all, **Spinosaurus** was a ferocious-looking beast. Herbivores such as **Triceratops** had to be constantly on the lookout.

CRETACEOUS

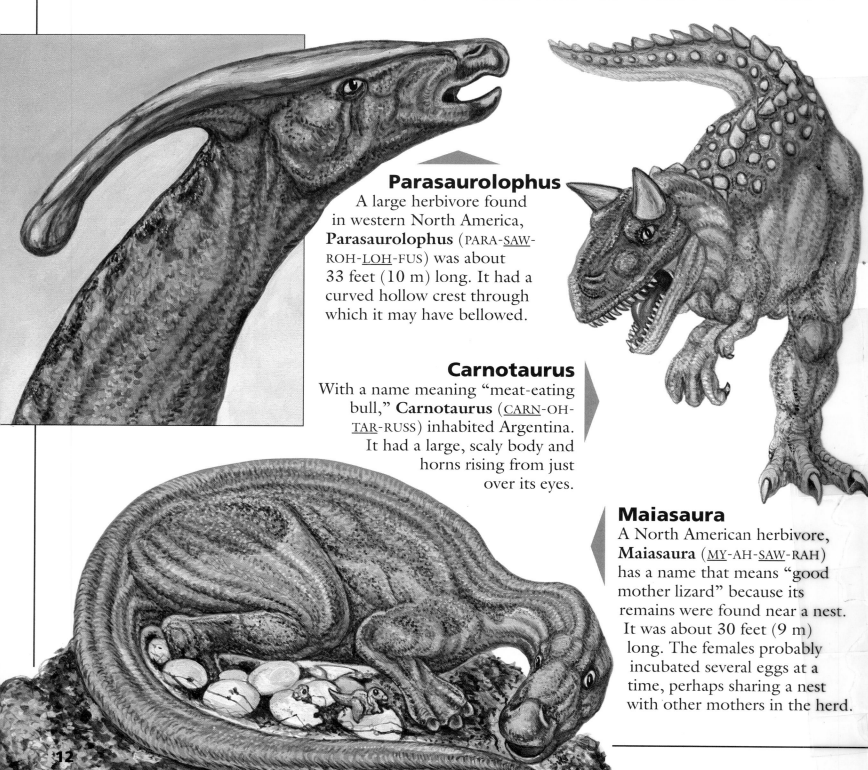

Parasaurolophus

A large herbivore found in western North America, **Parasaurolophus** (PARA-SAW-ROH-LOH-FUS) was about 33 feet (10 m) long. It had a curved hollow crest through which it may have bellowed.

Carnotaurus

With a name meaning "meat-eating bull," **Carnotaurus** (CARN-OH-TAR-RUSS) inhabited Argentina. It had a large, scaly body and horns rising from just over its eyes.

Maiasaura

A North American herbivore, **Maiasaura** (MY-AH-SAW-RAH) has a name that means "good mother lizard" because its remains were found near a nest. It was about 30 feet (9 m) long. The females probably incubated several eggs at a time, perhaps sharing a nest with other mothers in the herd.

GALLERY-1

Velociraptor

Known from remains discovered in China and Mongolia, **Velociraptor** (VEL-<u>AH</u>-SI-<u>RAP</u>-TOR) was very small by dinosaur standards, but still a fierce predator. The large, retractable claw on each foot must have been useful when **Velociraptor** needed to slash at prey.

Ankylosaurus

Mighty **Ankylosaurus** (AN-KILL-OH-<u>SAW</u>-RUS) was a well-armored plant-eater from what is now Alberta, Canada, and Montana in the United States. Paleontologists have described this 35-foot (11-m)-long dinosaur as a "living tank." It could have fought well against ferocious dinosaurs such as **Tyrannosaurus rex** by using its powerful clubbed tail — unless the hungry carnivore attacked **Ankylosaurus**'s soft belly.

13

CRETACEOUS

Ouranosaurus

Plant-eating **Ouranosaurus** (OO-<u>RAN</u>-OH-<u>SAW</u>-RUS) lived in what is now Niger, in Africa. It had an amazing sail 23 feet (7 m) long on its back and tail that perhaps played a role in its body temperature control.

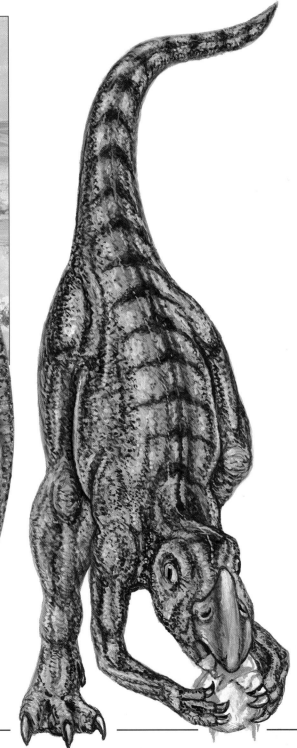

Iguanodon

A large herbivore able to walk on two legs or four, **Iguanodon** (IG-<u>WAHN</u>-OH-DON) lived in Europe, North America, and Mongolia. It had a toothless beak and spiked thumbs, probably for defense.

14

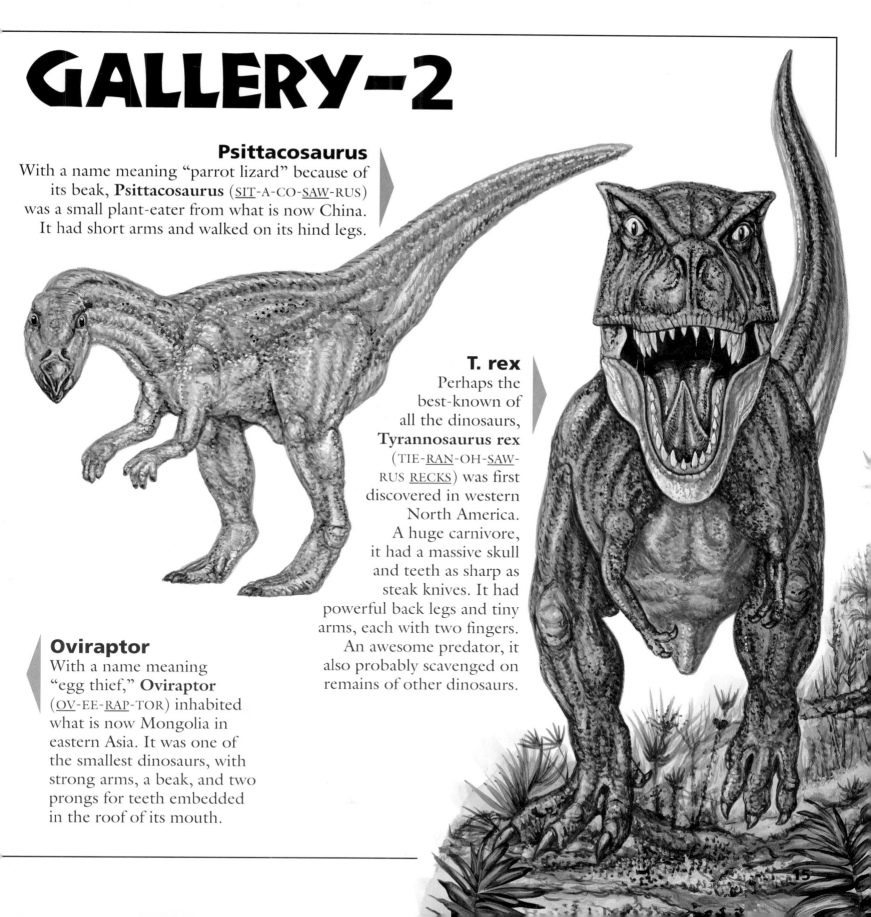

GALLERY-2

Psittacosaurus

With a name meaning "parrot lizard" because of its beak, **Psittacosaurus** (<u>SIT</u>-A-CO-<u>SAW</u>-RUS) was a small plant-eater from what is now China. It had short arms and walked on its hind legs.

T. rex

Perhaps the best-known of all the dinosaurs, **Tyrannosaurus rex** (TIE-<u>RAN</u>-OH-<u>SAW</u>-RUS <u>RECKS</u>) was first discovered in western North America. A huge carnivore, it had a massive skull and teeth as sharp as steak knives. It had powerful back legs and tiny arms, each with two fingers. An awesome predator, it also probably scavenged on remains of other dinosaurs.

Oviraptor

With a name meaning "egg thief," **Oviraptor** (<u>OV</u>-EE-<u>RAP</u>-TOR) inhabited what is now Mongolia in eastern Asia. It was one of the smallest dinosaurs, with strong arms, a beak, and two prongs for teeth embedded in the roof of its mouth.

15

CRETACEOUS

Baryonyx

Fossilized remains in the stomach cavity of **Baryonyx** (BARRY-<u>ON</u>-ICKS) led scientists to believe it ate fish. Found in England and 30 feet (9 m) long, its large thumb claws were possibly used for spearing food.

Muttaburrasaurus

Found in Australia, **Muttaburrasaurus** (MUTT-A-BUHR-AH-<u>SAW</u>-RUS) was a large plant-eater with a prominent muzzle, hooflike feet, and thumb spikes for self-defense.

Gallimimus

One of the speediest dinosaurs, ostrichlike **Gallimimus** (<u>GAL</u>-EE-<u>MIME</u>-US) was 20 feet (6 m) long. It lived in Mongolia and had clawed hands, slim legs, and a stiff tail that was held out behind as it ran.

GALLERY-3

Deinonychus

Deinonychus (DIE-NOH-<u>NEYE</u>-KUS) was a predatory dinosaur from western North America and was about 10 feet (3 m) long. Its name means "terrible claw" because of the large, switchblade killer claw it had on each foot.

Protoceratops

Native to Mongolia, **Protoceratops** (<u>PROH</u>-TOE-<u>SERA</u>-TOPS) was a plant-eater with a parrotlike beak and large head frill. It was only about 6 feet (2 m) long.

Pachycephalosaurus

A two-legged plant-eater, or herbivore, from North America, **Pachycephalosaurus** (<u>PACK</u>-EE-<u>SEF</u>-A-LOW-<u>SAW</u>-RUS) was about 15 feet (5 m) long. It used its thick, domed skull in head-to-head fights with others of the species.

17

BONEHEADS

One of the most amazing Cretaceous sights must have been a prehistoric head-to-head battle, when two dinosaurs of the same species challenged each other in head-butting contests.

Crunch! There was a loud noise as the two **Pachycephalosaurus** heads collided. Their skulls were so tough, however, that the blow hardly hurt either of them. Confidently, they stood back and then charged again. Boom! This time, one of the great creatures felt stunned. Having lost the urge for a further clash of heads, it stumbled away, defeated.

Ritual display
Most of this head-butting was a kind of social ritual. Once superiority had been established, the event would be over. Such clashes were usually between males, to determine social status and decide which would have first choice of the available females.

Pachycephalosaurus — its name means "thick-headed reptile" — lived in what is now North America. It stood upright and grew to about 26 feet (8 m) in height. It could withstand these head-to-head fights without sustaining brain damage because its skull was up to 10 inches (25 centimeters) thick.

Many other dinosaurs also had bony heads that allowed them to compete head-to-head, usually without suffering any serious damage. For example, **Stegoceras**, whose name means "horny roof," was just 8 feet (2.5 m) long, but had a domed head that grew stronger as it got older.

Stygimoloch was another type of pachycephalosaur.

It had long spikes around its head that acted as a form of display to other members of its species. Some experts think the length of the spikes may, at times, have been enough to establish social status — without a fight.

Most of the time, these bone-heads lived peacefully; it must have been startling when a contest began.

19

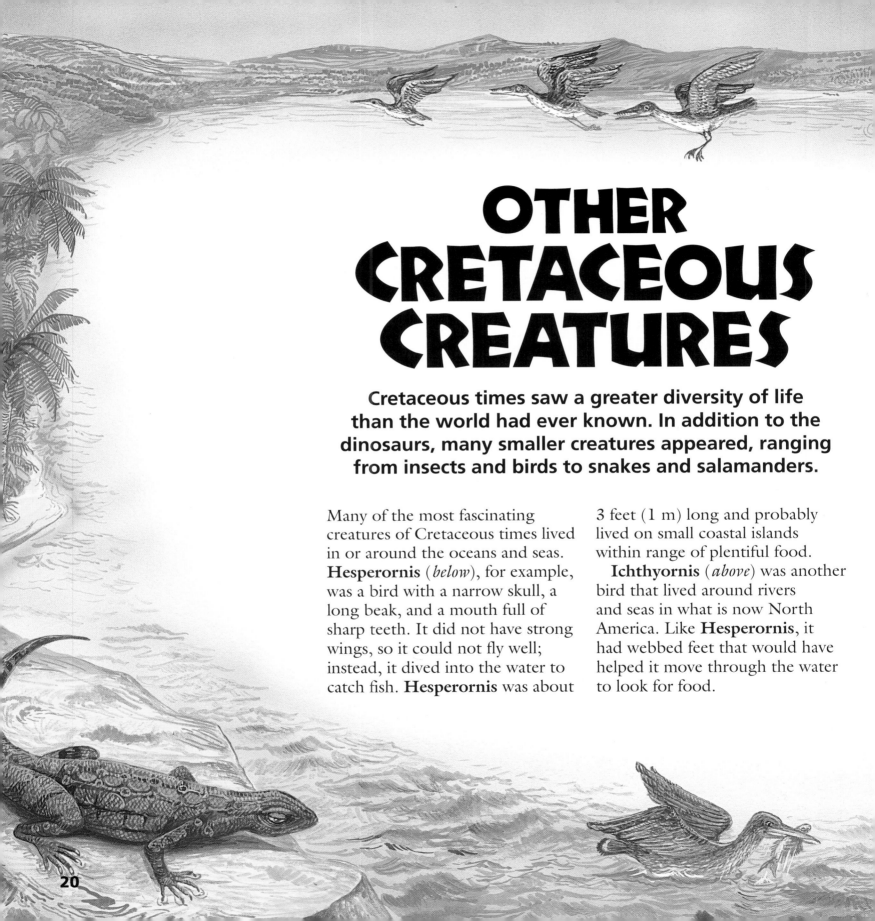

OTHER CRETACEOUS CREATURES

Cretaceous times saw a greater diversity of life than the world had ever known. In addition to the dinosaurs, many smaller creatures appeared, ranging from insects and birds to snakes and salamanders.

Many of the most fascinating creatures of Cretaceous times lived in or around the oceans and seas. **Hesperornis** (*below*), for example, was a bird with a narrow skull, a long beak, and a mouth full of sharp teeth. It did not have strong wings, so it could not fly well; instead, it dived into the water to catch fish. **Hesperornis** was about 3 feet (1 m) long and probably lived on small coastal islands within range of plentiful food.

Ichthyornis (*above*) was another bird that lived around rivers and seas in what is now North America. Like **Hesperornis**, it had webbed feet that would have helped it move through the water to look for food.

Ichthyornis was small, no bigger than a pigeon. Its remains show that it had a large rib cage, probably containing muscles that helped it fly. Just as **Hesperornis** did, **Ichthyornis** probably lived in colonies and hunted for fish.

Lost mammals

Multituberculates were early, rodentlike mammals. The name refers to their teeth, which had many "tubercles," or nodules, arranged in rows. These creatures have long been extinct, in spite of having flourished for about 100 million years in prehistoric times — much longer than any other mammal has existed either before or since.

Among this group were tiny, mouselike creatures, as well as slightly larger mammals that lived in burrows or trees. The largest multituberculates were as big as beavers (*bottom, right*).

Many Cretaceous animals, such as turtles, frogs, and lizards, looked very similar to those we know today. More crocodilians existed during this prehistoric time than exist now. **Deinosuchus**, which means "terrible crocodile," was the largest crocodile known. Its skull alone was 6 feet (1.8 m) long, so it may have snapped up dinosaurs in its jaws. The warm, damp conditions in Cretaceous times were ideal for this carnivorous animal.

THE CRETACEOUS DAY

As a new day dawned on Cretaceous Asia-America, a prehistoric landmass that included what is now eastern Asia and western North America, dinosaurs inevitably began their daily search for food. They were impatient for meals, and some could get very aggressive when hungry.

A hungry pack of **Troodon** spotted a potential victim across the river. It was a stray **Parasaurolophus**, searching drowsily for water plants. Soon, the **Troodon** — intelligent animals — would break cover and try to devise a means of attack. **Parasaurolophus**'s best hope for escape might be to head for the deeper water and swim to safety. It could also use its huge head crest to sound an alert. If no other creatures came to see what was going on, the mighty honk from its horn might at least frighten its attackers away.

Pack attacks

Like all the duck-billed dinosaurs, **Parasaurolophus** was not a natural fighter. **Troodon**, whose name means "wounding tooth," was smaller, but vicious, with sharp claws on its hands and feet. It knew that it stood a better chance of victory if it attacked as part of a pack.

Many plant-eating dinosaurs also lived in herds. They traveled and ate together throughout each Cretaceous day. They were social creatures that looked after their young very well, with a close family life that helped protect them against predators.

Cretaceous carnivores, on the other hand, had all the teeth, claws, and brute strength their predatory lifestyles demanded. But these meat-eaters did not kill unless they were hungry.

Eggs and babies, however, would have been too tasty to pass up if they saw an opportunity. Some, such as **Baryonyx**, may also have caught fish with their hooked claws.

Basic instincts

Dinosaurs had plenty to occupy their time during the Cretaceous day. They had to satisfy their basic instincts of eating, mating, battling over territory, and avoiding predators.

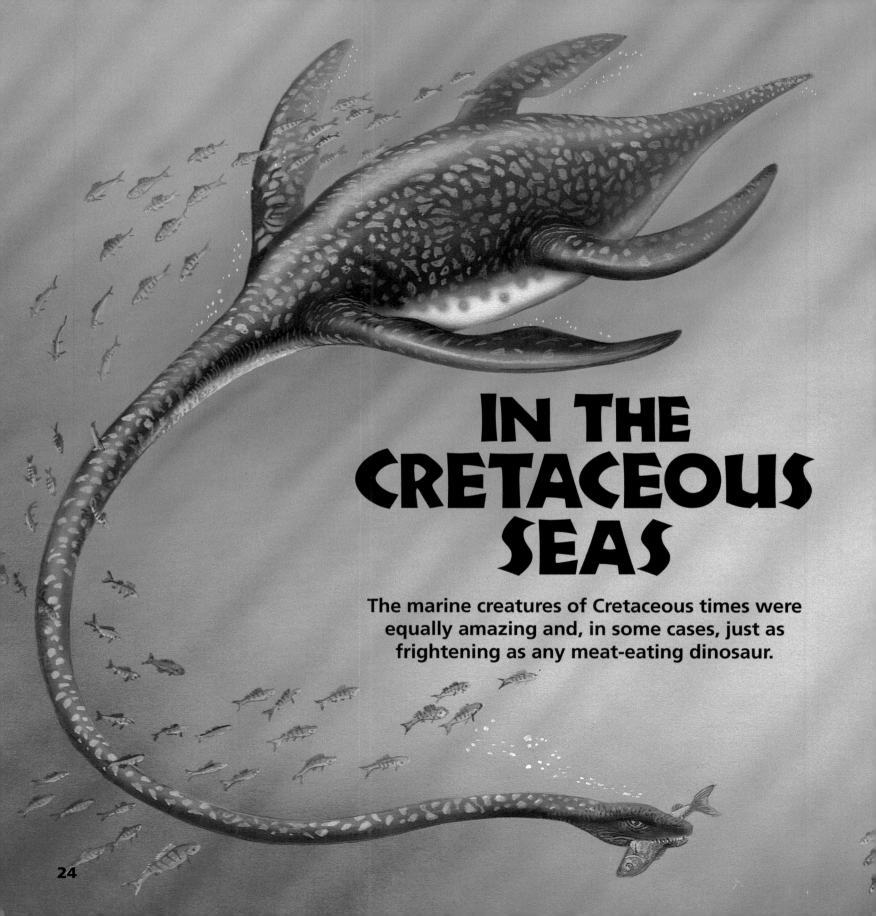

IN THE CRETACEOUS SEAS

The marine creatures of Cretaceous times were equally amazing and, in some cases, just as frightening as any meat-eating dinosaur.

Long-necked **Elasmosaurus** (*opposite*) greedily snatched a passing fish from the murky ocean waters. It swam off to enjoy the feast in a quieter spot, the fish tightly held within its snappy jaws. Nearby, a stockier, fiercer-looking creature, known as **Mosasaurus** (*below*), had opened its massive mouth and was preparing to devour an entire shoal of fish.

Territorial battles

In the never-ending search for food, these huge sea creatures may even have fought each other at times over the right to swim in the same stretch of water. Underwater territory was just as important to these inhabitants of the sea as dry land was for the dinosaurs.

Elasmosaurus belonged to the plesiosaur family. It grew to about 43 feet (13 m) in length, had a small head containing many sharp teeth, and had paddlelike limbs for propelling itself through the water. In all, there were seventy-six bones in its neck, more than any other creature that has ever lived! In fact, it could coil its long neck like a snake. Then, when it spotted a fish at a distance, it would swiftly uncoil its neck and pounce. It may even have emerged from the water at times to grab small flying reptiles.

Sea lizard

At 30 feet (9 m) in length, **Mosasaurus** was not as long as **Elasmosaurus**. But, with a thicker body and a longer snout, it was an altogether more frightening creature. Today's monitor lizards are distant relatives of Mosasaurus, which belonged to the mosasaur, "sea lizard," family. It used its powerful tail, paddlelike limbs, and sharp teeth to hunt fish, and stayed close to the water's surface while in pursuit of prey.

Underwater speed kings

The most graceful Cretaceous sea creatures of all were undoubtedly the ichthyosaurs. They resembled today's dolphins and swam at speeds of up to 25 miles (40 kilometers) per hour. Turtles were also fairly common in the seas at this time. They were, in fact, among the few species of prehistoric creatures that managed to survive the devastation which led to the mysterious death of the mighty dinosaurs 65 million years ago.

IN THE CRETACEOUS SKIES

Early species of birds flew over the Cretaceous landscape, but pterosaurs, or "winged lizards," were supreme in the skies. These powerful reptiles had strong muscles and huge wingspans that helped them stay high in the sky.

A noisy flock of squawking pterosaurs made the curious dinosaurs look up cautiously, but they did not need to be afraid. Pterosaurs were scavengers rather than hunters. They preferred feeding off dead bodies or catching fish and other seafood.

What, then, were the Cretaceous flying reptiles actually like? Their giant wings, made of leathery skin, were attached to limbs that ended in fingers. They would launch themselves off cliffs, like humans in hang gliders, in order to catch rising air currents. They had long beaks and large eyes that enabled them to spot food or danger at a distance.

The largest, **Quetzalcoatlus** (*center*), weighed about 220 pounds (100 kilograms), with a wingspan of about 40 feet (12 m). What strong muscles it must have had to help it fly!

Toothless fliers

Smaller **Pteranodon** (*below*) had a wingspan averaging about 23 feet (7 m), and it shared the skies with **Quetzalcoatlus** in North America. Scientists think **Pteranodon** was a master at catching fish in its large beak and swallowing them whole. It had no teeth, a feature referred to by its name, which means "toothless flyer."

Some types of **Pteranodon**, such as the one *opposite, right*, had distinctive head crests. **Pteranodon** may have used its crest as a rudder for balance when soaring in the sky, swooping down to catch fish, or skimming quickly over the water's surface. Most pterosaurs were definitely more comfortable flying than walking on land, where they were probably inhibited by their wings.

These reptiles would have laid their eggs

on cliffs, however, where they gathered as part of a colony.

Many pterosaur remains have been found inland — evidence, perhaps, of what powerful fliers they must have been.

Following their extinction at the end of Cretaceous times, the skies were never again filled with such huge creatures.

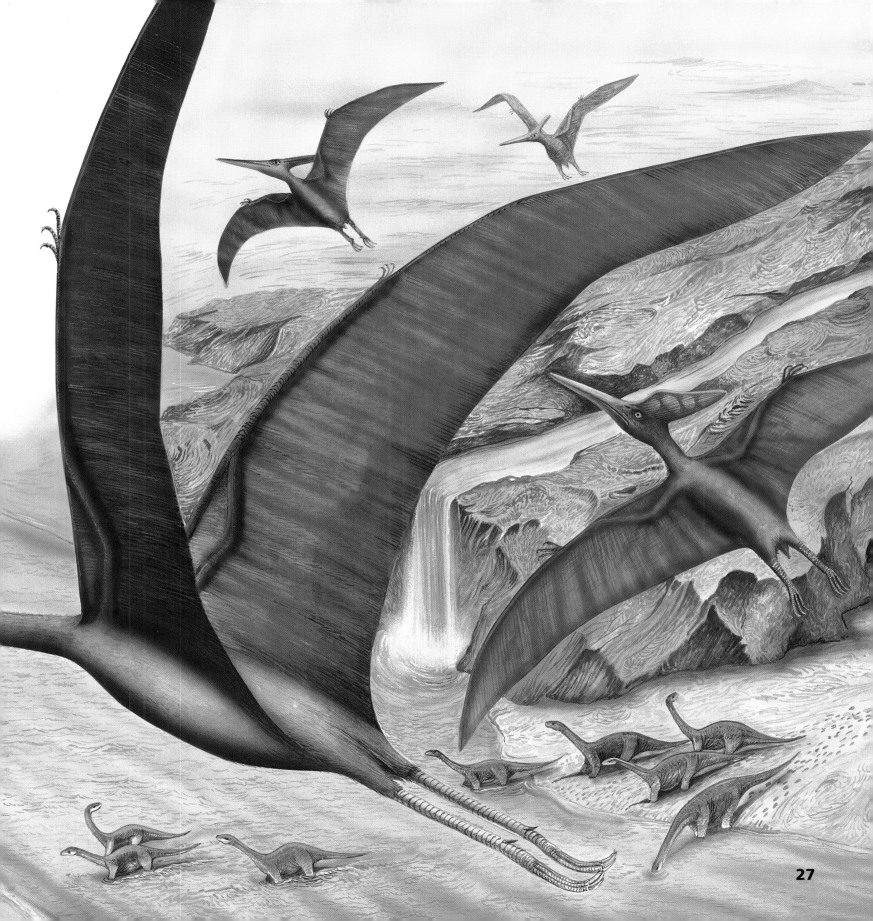

DEMISE OF THE DINOSAURS

Dinosaurs flourished for some 150 million years, much longer than human beings have existed. About 65 million years ago, however, something happened that heralded the beginning of the end of their species.

Never since life had first appeared on Earth had such scenes of destruction occurred. Dinosaurs ran in all directions. Even the largest carnivores were terrified. Herbivorous **Triceratops** thundered across the plains, roaring in panic, as fireballs rained down on Earth. Pterosaurs risked being burned to a crisp as they flew. The sky had turned a reddish-black color, and it seemed as if the planet might split apart.

Debate has raged among scientists for many years as to what actually caused the extinction of the dinosaurs. One theory was that a virus wiped them out; another, that small mammals ate all the dinosaur eggs. Some have argued that the dinosaurs became too large to mate, or that they were unable to adapt to the changing climate, but this ignores their diversity and success in surviving for so many millions of years.

Crash-landing

Today, however, most paleontologists agree that a giant asteroid about 6 miles (10 km) in diameter crash-landed on our planet at a site in what is now Mexico. A large crater, some 180 miles (290 km) wide, has been found at a place called Chiczulub, which is known to have been rich in sulfur. The rocks found in that area are full of material usually associated with asteroids and comets. The explosion caused by such a terrific crash would have sent clouds of poisonous substances, such as sulfur, into the atmosphere.

Eventually, a thick haze would have settled above Earth, blocking the sunlight and creating a long, cold period that may have lasted for years. Without sunlight, the plants would have died, which would have led to gradual starvation for the herbivores.

As their numbers decreased, the carnivores, in turn, would have had fewer creatures to hunt and eat. The meat-eaters, too, would have eventually died out.

This did not happen overnight, of course. In fact, it may have taken several thousands of years for the dinosaurs to disappear entirely. Without the death of the dinosaurs, however, perhaps the human race might never have evolved to survive as it has.

GLOSSARY

asteroid — one of the thousands of small planets that orbit the sun between Mars and Jupiter.

carnivore — a meat-eater.

convulse — to violently shake or stir something up.

Cretaceous times — the final era of the dinosaurs, lasting from 144–65 million years ago.

crocodilians — animals belonging to the crocodile family.

evolved — adapted and changed over a long period of time to suit changing environments.

foliage — the leaves of a tree, shrub, or plant.

fossilized — embedded and preserved in rocks, resin, or other material.

frill — a head shield, formed of bone, probably used to protect certain dinosaurs from attack or to scare enemies, and, on the males of some species, to attract females.

hadrosaurs — members of a group of duck-billed dinosaurs.

herbivore — a plant-eater.

ichthyosaurs — extinct marine reptiles that had fishlike bodies and long snouts.

incubate — to warm and protect eggs until it is time for the young to hatch.

instinct — a way of behaving that is natural, or automatic, rather than learned.

Jurassic times — the middle era of the dinosaurs, lasting from 213–144 million years ago.

localized — limited or restricted to certain areas.

marine — related to the ocean or sea.

mosasaurs — large, fish-eating reptiles that lived in the prehistoric seas, related to today's monitor lizards.

multituberculates — members of a group of rodentlike mammals that lived about 100 million years ago.

paleontologist — a scientist who studies past geologic periods as they are known from fossil remains.

plesiosaurs — long-necked, prehistoric marine reptiles.

predator — an animal that hunts other animals for food.

primitive — in an early stage of development; not highly developed or evolved.

pterosaurs — members of a group of extinct flying reptiles.

retractable — able to be drawn in or pulled back in, like the claws of some animals.

salamanders — members of a group of amphibians that look like lizards, but instead have moist, smooth skin.

sauropods — members of a group of long-necked, plant-eating dinosaurs with small heads and five-toed feet.

scavenge — to eat the leftovers or carcasses of other animals.

sulfur — a pale yellow substance that burns with a blue flame and produces a strong, unpleasant smell.

Triassic times — the first era of the dinosaurs, lasting from 249–213 million years ago.

tubercles — small, rounded nodules, or lumps, such as those found on the teeth of the prehistoric, rodentlike mammals called multituberculates.

volatile — easily changeable; explosive.

MORE BOOKS TO READ

Death From Space: What Killed the Dinosaurs?
  Isaac Asimov and Greg Walz-Chojnacki
  (Gareth Stevens)

Dinosaur Dinners. Barbara Taylor
  (Dorling Kindersley)

Dinosaurs. David Norman (Knopf)

Draw, Model, and Paint (series): *Dinosaurs*
  (3 of 6 vols.). Isidro Sanchez (Gareth Stevens)

The Extinction of Dinosaurs. Dan Nardo
  (Lucent Books)

*Looking at Tyrannosaurus rex: A Dinosaur from
  the Cretaceous Period.* Heather Amery
  (Gareth Stevens)

The New Dinosaur Collection (series).
  (Gareth Stevens)

World of Dinosaurs (series). (Gareth Stevens)

VIDEOS

All About Dinosaurs. (United Learning)

Did Comets Kill The Dinosaurs? (Gareth Stevens)

Digging Up Dinosaurs. (Great Plains National
  Instructional Television Library)

Dinosaur! (series). (Arts & Entertainment Network)

Dinosaurs: The Age of Reptiles.
  (Phoenix/BFA Films & Video)

Dinosaurs: Remains to Be Seen. (Public Media, Inc.)

Dinosaurs: The Terrible Lizards. (AIMS Media)

The Last Word on Dinosaurs.
  (Films for the Humanities and Sciences)

More Dinosaurs. (Twin Tower Enterprises)

Nova: The Case of the Flying Dinosaur.
  (Live Home Video)

WEB SITES

pubs.usgs.gov/gip/dinosaurs/

www.ZoomDinosaurs.com/

www.fmnh.org

www.dinosociety.org

www.ucmp.berkeley.edu/diapsids/dinosaur.html

www.dinofest.org/kids/kids.html

Due to the dynamic nature of the Internet, some web sites stay current longer than others. To find additional web sites, use a reliable search engine with one or more of the following keywords to help you locate more information about dinosaurs. Keywords: *Cretaceous, dinosaurs, fossils, Jurassic, paleontology, prehistoric, Triassic.*

INDEX